Dropping In On...
NEW ZEALAND

Christina J. Moose

A Geography Series

THE ROURKE BOOK COMPANY, INC.
VERO BEACH, FLORIDA 32964

Printed in the United States of America

**Library of Congress
Cataloging-in-Publication Data**

Moose, Christina J., 1952-
  New Zealand / Christina J. Moose.
    p. cm. — (Dropping in on)
  Includes bibliographical references and index.
  ISBN 1-55916-283-X
  1. New Zealand—Juvenile literature. [1. New Zealand—
  Description and travel.] I. Title. II. Series.

DU408 .M66 2000
993—dc21
                                    00–029071

New Zealand
■ ■ ■ ■ ■ ■ ■ ■ ■ ■ ■ ■ ■ ■ ■ ■ ■

Official Name: New Zealand (English),
Aotearoa (Maori)

Area: 104,440 square miles
(270,534 square kilometers)

Population: 3.8 million

Capital: Wellington

Largest City: Auckland
(population 1,060,000)

Highest Elevation: Mount Cook,
12,349 feet (3,764 meters)

Official Languages: English, Maori

Major Religion: Christian (81%)

Money: New Zealand dollar

Form of Government:
Constitutional monarchy

Flag:

TABLE OF CONTENTS

Our Blue Ball—The Earth

The Earth can be divided into two hemispheres. The word hemisphere means "half a ball"—in this case, the ball is the Earth.

The equator is an imaginary line that runs around the middle of the Earth. It separates the Northern Hemisphere from the Southern Hemisphere. North America—where Canada, the United States, and Mexico are located—is in the Northern Hemisphere.

The Southern Hemisphere

When the South Pole is tilted toward the sun, the sun's most powerful rays strike the southern half of the Earth and less sunshine hits the Northern Hemisphere. That is when people in the Southern Hemisphere enjoy summer. When the South Pole is tilted away from the sun and the Northern Hemisphere receives the most sunshine, the seasons reverse. Then winter comes to the Southern Hemisphere. The seasons in the Southern Hemisphere and the Northern Hemisphere are always opposite.

Get Ready for New Zealand

Let's take a trip! Climb into your hot-air balloon, and we'll drop in on a country of glaciers, mountains, lakes, volcanoes, and bubbling mud. It is also a land of sandy beaches, rolling hills, baa-ing sheep, and friendly people who call themselves "Kiwis," after the national bird.

New Zealand is really two big islands. Together they look like an upside-down boot. North Island is the "foot" of the boot, and South Island is the "leg." Along with Stewart Island in the far south and many smaller islands, New Zealand is about the size of Colorado: about 1,000 miles (1,600 kilometers) from north to south and no more than 280 miles (450 kilometers) at the widest point.

Millions of years ago, in the South Pacific Ocean north of Antarctica and east of Australia, the edge of a *continental plate* (a section of Earth's crust) pushed against another continental plate and bulged up out of the water. Volcanoes formed when hot liquid rocks, called *lava*, spurted up between the plates. The lava cooled and made more land, building tall mountains. New Zealand was born.

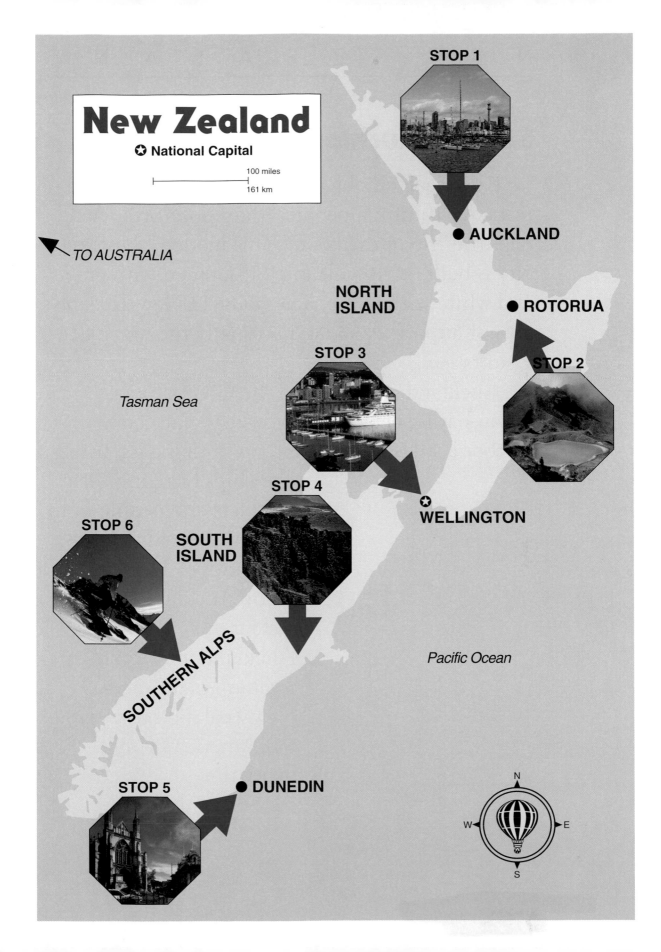

Stop 1: Auckland

New Zealand's biggest city is Auckland, with just over 1 million people. It lies on North Island near the "tip of the boot." This modern, bustling city is built on 46 volcanic hills, green with grass and white with sheep. The home of New Zealand's busiest airport, Auckland is usually the first place visitors see.

Auckland is also called the City of Sails, because it is surrounded by water. Waitemata Harbor is filled with thousands of sailboats, barges, and ships bringing products and people from Asia, the Pacific islands, and Europe. They come to enjoy Auckland's beaches, restaurants, and shops. Aucklanders often host *regattas* (yacht races). New Zealand has won the America's Cup many times.

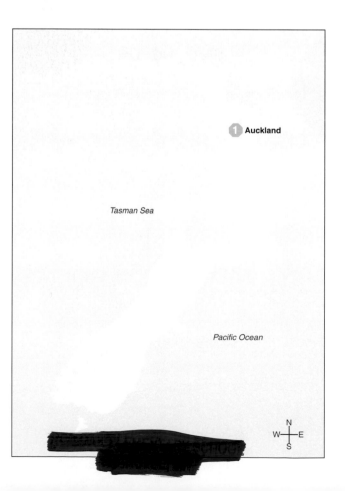

1 Auckland

Tasman Sea

Pacific Ocean

*Now let's fly **south** to Rotorua.*

Above: Auckland is the first sight many visitors to New Zealand see. Inset: On North Island, giant kauri trees can grow ten stories tall and live for a thousand years.

The Maori People

One thousand years ago, a man named Kupe led a group of island people called *Polynesians* to New Zealand. They settled mainly on North Island, where the weather is mild. Then, 300 years ago, Europeans from England started their own towns in New Zealand. The Polynesians began to call themselves *Maori* (MOH-ree), which means "normal people." They called the Europeans *Pakeha* (PAA-ke-ha), which means "white strangers."

The Europeans brought strange new diseases, and many Maoris died. Later the Maoris grew strong again. Today almost one-sixth (15%) of New Zealand's population is Maori. Some Maoris are mixed, with both European and Maori ancestors.

The Maori people love to celebrate their *Maoritanga* (Maori culture). Maoris still wear traditional tattoos called *mokos* (MOR-kors). They worship in *Ratana* and *Ringatu* churches, and they have their own seats in New Zealand's House of Representatives.

Maoris are admired as wood sculptors, weavers, and *tukutuku* artists who create geometric designs

Above: The Maori people crossed the oceans to reach New Zealand one thousand years ago.

Right: A traditional Maori wood carving.

from colored reeds. The national rugby team dances a Maori war dance, the *haka* (HUH-kuh), before a game. Maoris even have a special name for New Zealand: *Aotearoa* (ah-or-te-ah-roar), Land of the Long White Cloud.

Hot springs in Tongariro National Park, North Island.

Stop 2: Rotorua

A *geyser* is a fountain of boiling water that explodes into the sky from deep inside the Earth. Only a few places in the world have geysers. One of them is in New Zealand. A trail of geysers, volcanoes, bubbling mud pools, and hot springs runs from the middle of North Island to the Bay of Plenty. Years ago, one of the volcanoes erupted, making a hole 230 miles (600 kilometers) square. This *crater* became Lake Taupo.

The town of Rotorua (roh-toh-ROO-rah), north of Lake Taupo, attracts many visitors. As they drive toward Rotorua they can see steam rising from holes in the ground. The Maori people once used these steam holes to cook their food. The air smells like rotten eggs. People in Rotorua can hear their gardens hissing!

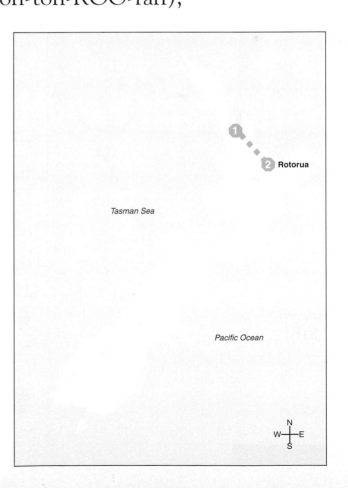

*Now let's fly **south** again to Wellington.*

Stop 3: Wellington

About 400,000 people live in Wellington, the capital of New Zealand. "Windy Wellington" sits on the Cook Strait, the channel of water between North and South Islands. The writer Katherine Mansfield was born in a house that still stands in Wellington, and the world-famous soprano Dame Kiri Te Kanawa, born in Gisborne, sometimes sings at Wellington's Opera House. Wellington is also the birthplace of the actress Anna Paquin, who won an Academy Award when she was only eleven years old for her role in the movie *The Piano*.

Wellington is the seat of New Zealand's government. The old Government Building, one of the largest wooden structures ever built, is used by the university.

Now let's fly **south** to South Island.

Wellington's harbor.

Inset: Te Papa, New Zealand's national museum, opened in Wellington in 1998. It has a room that shakes like an earthquake.

Growing Up in New Zealand

Most children in New Zealand grow up in small towns, with both a mother and father and often one brother or sister—although today many families may have only one child. Nearly all children go to school from the ages of five through sixteen, and many go on to trade school or university. Maori children can go to schools that teach lessons in their own language.

Children who grow up in rural areas, far from the cities, can learn through the Correspondence School. *Correspondence* means "communication at a distance." Children can take their lessons at home, far away from the school. Rural children may also worship in their church or *marae* (a Maori spiritual and social center), participate in "agricultural and pastoral" (A&P) festivals, compete in sheep-shearing contests, and work on the farm.

Kiwi kids love the outdoors: *tramping* (hiking) in the mountains, sailing on the ocean, kayaking in the rivers, or biking through the green country-side. In Queenstown on South Island, they can learn to ski. They also enjoy the national sport, a type of football called *rugby*.

Above: Rugby, a type of football, is New Zealand's national sport.
Below: Rafting is one of many outdoor activities.

Stop 4: South Island

Only one-quarter of New Zealand's people live on South Island. Except for the northern tip of the island, where wine makers grow grapes near Marlborough Sounds, South Island is colder, wilder, and more rural than North Island.

South Island's rugged beauty can startle first-time visitors. Off the west coast, where miners once dug for gold, the sun can be shining on snow-capped peaks. Then suddenly a storm can dump snow and ice on the mountaintops and rain on the forests below.

Along the eastern side are fertile plains and the island's biggest city, Christchurch (320,000 people). Smaller cities like Akaroa, Dunedin, and Invercargill lie to the south. Here, sheep and cattle graze on the grassy slopes above the plains.

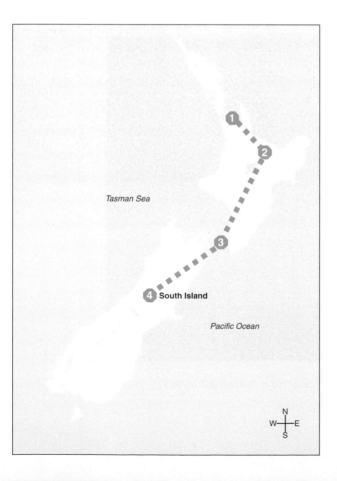

*Now let's fly **south** to Dunedin.*

The West Coast of South Island is wild and rough.

Stop 5: Dunedin

One of South Island's most interesting towns is Dunedin, on the Otago Peninsula. Dunedin (dun-EE-din) is called the "Edinburgh of the South" because it has the same name as the ancient Scottish city, Dun Edin. Many of Dunedin's 120,000 people are students who attend its university. Dunedin is known for its Scottish heritage, its castles, and its rock bands.

The Otago Peninsula is a *sanctuary* (safe place) for penguins, seals, and other wildlife. At the tip of the peninsula, at Taiaroa Head, is a breeding area for the royal albatross, one of the largest birds in the world. When these birds spread their wings to fly, they are 10 feet (3 meters) wide!

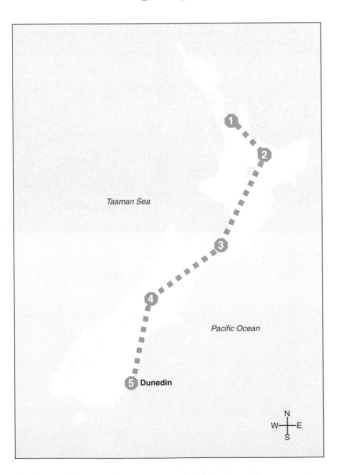

*Now let's fly **north-west** to the Southern Alps.*

Saint Paul's Cathedral and Town Hall in Dunedin.

Kiwi Country

New Zealand is home to some unusual animals, including several flightless birds—birds that cannot fly. The ostrich-sized moa is now extinct, but it lived 1,000 years ago and grew to be 10 feet (3 meters) tall. Other flightless birds still live in New Zealand: the *takahe*, the *weka*, and the *kakapo*, the heaviest parrot in the world.

Another of these birds, the *kiwi*, has become a national symbol for New Zealand. The kiwi is shy and comes out only at night. It is shaped like a pear, with a long, needle-like bill. Most birds have nostrils at the top of the bill, but the kiwi's nostrils are at the end of its bill. Kiwis lay eggs that are very big, about one-third the size of the mother. The father takes care of these eggs until they hatch.

New Zealanders are fond of the kiwi bird. They have a picture of the kiwi on their dollar coin. They grow a green fruit, with a hairy brown skin, called "kiwi fruit." They even call themselves "Kiwis"!

The shy kiwi bird is one of New Zealand's national symbols.

Stop 6: The Southern Alps

The Southern Alps run like a spine down the west coast of South Island. They hold more than 360 *glaciers*. These deep rivers of ice are always frozen but move slowly, carving out valleys and *fjords* (deep, narrow lakes). The biggest one, Tasman Glacier, is 18 miles (29 kilometers) long. Sixteen peaks rise above 10,000 feet (3,000 meters). The highest is Mount Cook (Mount Aoraki), at 12,349 feet (3,764 meters).

Fjordland National Park, at the southern end of the Alps, has some of the world's best hiking trails, such as the Milford Track. Fjordland is also one of the wettest regions in the world. From June through August, heavy rains fall on the mountains and help the forest's beech trees grow to a height of 100 feet (30 meters).

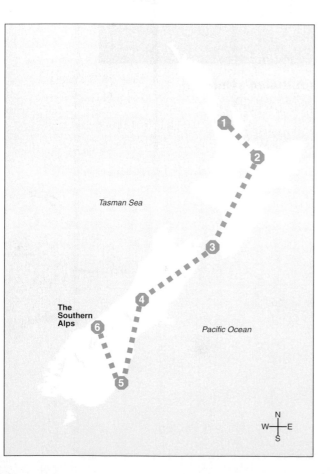

Now it is time to fly home.

Visitors to South Island's Tasman Glacier love to ski down the snowy slopes.

The Foods of New Zealand

New Zealand's people enjoy good food, mainly grown on their own farms or harvested from the sea. Because so many sheep and cattle graze in New Zealand's green pastures, dairy foods are an important part of the diet. Cheeses, milk, and cream are used in many dishes, and New Zealand's rich ice cream is world-famous. Kiwis also like fast foods such as fish 'n' chips: fish fried in batter and served with large french fries.

With so many rivers, lakes, and ocean waters, it is no surprise that meals often include green-shell mussels, *pipis* (clams), crayfish, snapper, salmon, and trout. Venison (deer meat) and lamb are popular meats, grilled with home-grown vegetables on the "barbie" (barbecue) during outdoor picnics.

Maori feasts also take place outdoors. A large pit, called a *hangi*, is filled with wood, piled with stones, and set on fire. Meat, fish, squash, and *kumara* (white sweet potatoes) are steamed on these stones. The people gather in the *marae* to eat, visit, tell stories, and dance.

29

Being close to the sea, it's no surprise that New Zealanders love eating fish.

Glossary

Aotearoa   The Maori name for New Zealand, meaning Land of the Long White Cloud.

crater   A huge hole made when a volcano erupts.

fjord   A deep, narrow lake, often carved by a glacier.

geyser   Boiling water that explodes from deep inside the Earth.

glacier   A deep river of ice that moves slowly, cutting valleys out of the land.

hangi   A large pit for cooking food. Also, the feast that follows.

kiwi   A shy, flightless bird found in New Zealand. Also, a nickname for a New Zealander (Kiwi).

Maori   The first people to arrive in New Zealand, from Pacific islands to the east.

Maoritanga   Maori culture.

marae   A social and spiritual center where Maori meet and celebrate.

Pakeha   The Maori word for Europeans.

Polynesians   People native to the central and southern Pacific islands.

rugby   The national sport of New Zealand, a type of football.

strait   A channel of water that runs between two masses of land.

tramping   Hiking.

tukutuku   A special Maori art using colored reeds to make designs.

Further Reading

Fox, Mary Virginia. *New Zealand*. Chicago: Childrens Press, 1991.

Griffiths, Jonathan. *New Zealand*. Milwaukee: Gareth Stevens, 1999.

Landau, Elaine. *Australia and New Zealand*. Chicago: Childrens Press, 1999.

Robson, Michael. *New Zealand in Pictures*. Minneapolis: Lerner Publications, 1990.

Smelt, Roselynn. *New Zealand*. Tarrytown, N.Y.: Marshall Cavendish Corporation, 1998.

Stevenson, Andrew. *Kiwi Tracks*. London: Lonely Planet, 1999.

Suggested Web Sites

Discover New Zealand Travel Guide
<http://www.new-zealand.com/nzguide/>

New Zealand Embassy
<http://www.nzemb.org/>

Te Papa, The National Museum of New Zealand
<http://www.tepapa.govt.nz/>

Index

Acknowledgments and Photo Credits
Cover: ©Richard Adams; pp. 11, 13, 21: © Robin Karpan. All other photos: Courtesy of New Zealand
Tourism Board.